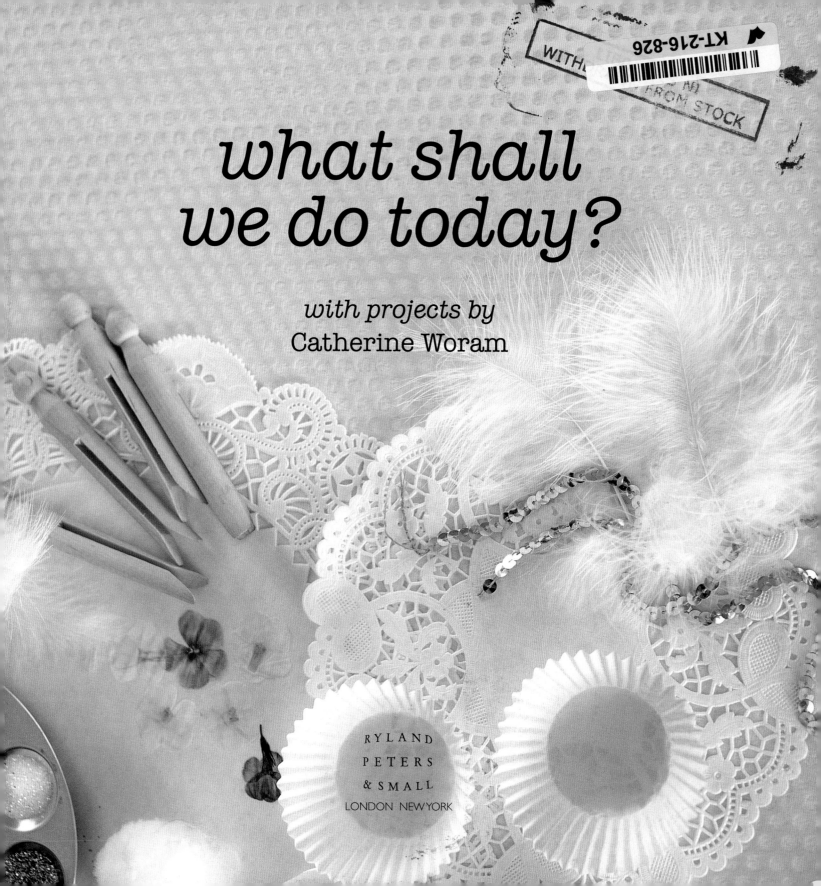

what shall we do today?

with projects by
Catherine Woram

RYLAND
PETERS
& SMALL
LONDON NEW YORK

Designer Iona Hoyle
Commissioning editor Annabel Morgan
Picture research Emily Westlake
Production Hazel Kirkman
Art director Leslie Harrington
Publishing director Alison Starling

Stylist Catherine Woram

First published in the UK in 2009
by Ryland Peters and Small
20–21 Jockey's Fields
London WC1R 4BW
www.rylandpeters.com

10 9 8 7 6 5 4 3 2 1

All the projects in this book are by Catherine Woram,
except the recipes on pages 26–27 and 126–127,
which are both by Linda Collister.
The projects in this book have been published
previously by Ryland Peters & Small in *Baking with
Kids*, *Christmas Crafting with Kids*, *Cooking with Kids*,
Crafting with Kids and *Gardening with Kids*.

ISBN: 978-1-84597-886-0

contents

6 | *introduction*

8 | **spring** Valentine's day card, Mother's Day gift, paper windmills, weaving, printed apron, painted eggs, garden tote, gingerbread people, pompoms, cress eggheads, découpage, paper flowers, tin can windchime, papier mâché dinosaur, wooden nesting box and wooden-spoon puppets.

48 | **summer** Funky fans, pressing flowers, painted stones, painted pots, modelling with balsa wood, herb planter, harvesting herbs, tie-dye t-shirt, crystallised flowers, split-pin animals, colourful annuals, father's day gift and pretty plant labels.

76 | **autumn** Peanut heart, covering books, indoor garden, finger puppets, modelling with clay, birdseed feeder, harvest wreath, cat mask, mirror-image painting, halloween hat, seed necklace, pretty seed packets, lavender bags, and a pumpkin lantern

106 | **winter** Twig decorations, orange tree decorations, paper snowflakes, pine cone animals, paper chains, finger-and hand-painting, felt motif cards, peppermint creams, pot pourri, Christmas spice cookies, snow shakers, potato print wrapping paper, nativity scene, orange pomanders, hanging felt stars, chocolate brownies, angel tree topper, and a Christmas stocking.

152 | *templates*

156 | *stockists*

158 | *picture credits*

158 | *index*

160 | *acknowledgements*

introduction

If you have kids, you'll know that they love pottering around with paint, scissors and glue. As well as providing an outlet for their creativity, crafting has educational benefits too. Modelling, cutting and painting will help develop hand-eye coordination, while learning to follow simple instructions is an important skill. And craft activities keep kids occupied and happy without having to resort to the TV or computer screen.

What Shall We Do Today? is packed with projects especially designed to appeal to children aged between 3 and 10 years. The book is arranged by season, and each section is full of ideas for crafting activities. There are suggestions for handmade gifts, things to grow and pretty decorations to make – absorbing projects that will keep kids entertained on long summer days and rainy afternoons alike. There's something for everyone – modelling, stencilling, papier mâché, tie-dye and much, much more. And each project is accompanied by step-by-step photos that simplify the technique and make the project foolproof.

If your kids are keen crafters, it's a good idea to put together a craft cupboard. Stock it with basic crafting materials – glue, sticky tape, paper and card, pencils and paint – and add scraps of wrapping paper or fabric, bits of ribbon, paper doilies, glitter pens and so on. Then, when your kids want to get crafting, they'll have everything they need right to hand.

spring

valentine's day card

This three-dimensional Valentine's Day card features hearts cut from decorative handmade paper. Tissue paper and paper doilies would also make pretty hearts for the card. Use pinking shears and decorative scissors (available from craft shops) to cut the paper, and finish with a ribbon bow.

1 DRAW HEARTS For the card, you need three heart shapes in decreasing sizes. Fold three pieces of decorative paper in half and press the crease flat. Draw half a heart shape in three different sizes onto each folded piece of decorative paper. Alternatively, you could trace the heart templates on page 152 onto paper and cut them out. Place the templates on your chosen paper and draw round them before cutting them out.

2 CUT OUT HEARTS Use the decorative cutting scissors or pinking shears to cut all the way around the edges of the heart motif, and then open it out flat. Cut out two smaller heart shapes in the same way. If you wish, you can cut out more hearts in graduating sizes to make an even more decorative card.

3 LAYER HEARTS Apply a line of glue down the centre of the back of the largest heart, stick to the middle of the card and press flat. Apply glue to the centre back of the smaller heart and glue to the first heart shape on the card. Apply the smallest heart in the same way. Allow the glue to dry.

4 FINISH OFF Using sheer organza or velvet ribbon, cut a bow and trim the ends diagonally to prevent the ribbon fraying. Apply a small dot of glue to the central knot of the bow and stick to the heart. Leave to dry. A matching ribbon looks pretty stuck onto the back of the envelope flap, too.

mother's day gift

This dainty decorated bowl is perfect for a Mother's Day gift. It uses the traditional papier mâché technique combined with layers of PVA glue, which means that the bowl can be created with fewer layers of paper to give a more delicate appearance.

1 COVER BOWL Place your bowl mould upside down on a flat surface and cover it with a layer of clingfilm. Tear the newspaper into strips. Paint over the clingfilm with a thin layer of PVA glue, then carefully apply the first layer of paper. Repeat this process until you have built up four layers of paper. Leave to dry overnight.

2 LIFT OFF PAPIER MÂCHÉ BOWL When it is completely dry, gently ease the papier mâché bowl away from the ceramic bowl and remove the clingfilm wrap. You can tidy the edges of the bowl with scissors, if desired.

3 PAINT THE BOWL Using a thick paintbrush, paint the bowl inside and out with the main colour. Allow to dry, then apply a further coat of paint. Leave to dry before applying the decoration to the bowl.

4 DECORATE We decorated the bowl with lilac and pink daisies. You may find it easier to draw the design on in pencil first. Leave to dry. A coat of water-based acrylic varnish will seal the paint and give a more hard-wearing finish.

paper windmills

Boys and girls alike will delight in making these colourful, old-fashioned windmills that twirl gaily in even the slightest breeze. Try making extra ones and stick them into flowerpots for fun party decorations.

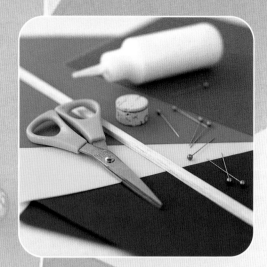

1 CHOOSE COLOURS Choose the colours of paper you are going to use to make the windmill. We used bold green, blue and yellow, but soft pastels or hot pink and zingy orange look great too.

2 GLUE AND CUT Apply a thin layer of glue to the back of one sheet of paper. Lay the other sheet on top and press flat. Rub gently, making sure there are no wrinkles or air bubbles trapped between the two sheets. Allow the glue to dry. Now, from the corner of each square, cut a line approx. 10cm long towards the centre of the paper.

3 FORM BLADES With the paper in front of you, gently bend every other point of the paper into the centre of the paper. Hold in place with your fingers until all four corners are folded into the centre.

4 SECURE WITH PIN Push a pin through the centre, making sure it goes through all four corners. It is advisable for an adult to do this. Push the pin into a cork. Using strong glue, attach the stick to the back of the cork, and allow to dry. Glue on a disc of card to hide the head of the pin, if desired.

weaving

Weaving is fun for most ages except the very young. The technique is easy to accomplish and can be applied to both two- and three-dimensional projects. Children will enjoy weaving cushions or bags from ribbons, or pen pots or boxes from coloured pipe-cleaners.

1 CUT THE RIBBON Cut the ribbon into 45cm lengths and divide into separate piles by colour. We used brightly coloured satin ribbon, although you could substitute pretty pastels or even fabric cut into narrow strips with a pair of pinking shears.

2 PIN ALONG EDGE Carefully arrange the ribbon lengths down one side of the fabric square, alternating two different colours. Pin the ribbons in place using one pin per length of ribbon to hold them firmly in place during weaving.

3 START WEAVING Take one of the remaining ribbon pieces and pin it to the adjacent side of the fabric square. Thread the ribbon over the first piece of ribbon and under the next and repeat until you reach the other side of the fabric square. Pin in place. Repeat with the other ribbon colour until the weaving is finished. Pin each piece of ribbon in place to stop it from slipping.

4 STITCH TO BASE Use a needle and thread to sew neatly all the way around the four sides of the woven ribbon square, stitching it firmly to the backing square.

printed apron

This fun gardening apron is printed with a design of apples, created using the traditional potato-printing method. The outline of the apple makes a simple, bold motif on the fabric. Use a ready-bought apron or make your own from calico and colourful bias binding.

1 APPLY PAINT TO STAMP
Ask a grown-up to cut the apple in half. Blot it with kitchen paper to remove excess moisture. Squirt some paint in a saucer, dip the paint roller in the paint and blot on side of plate to remove excess paint. Apply paint to the apple.

2 STAMP DESIGN ON APRON
Carefully place the apple cut-side down on the apron and press down firmly to make the imprint. Use a slight rocking motion to make sure the paint has been applied to the whole area, but be careful not to smudge the print.

3 FINISH OFF Using the roller, apply more paint to the apple, then repeat the design all around the apron, as desired. Allow the paint to dry thoroughly, then iron the apron to seal the paint (following the manufacturer's instructions).

WHAT YOU WILL NEED

- apple
- sharp knife for cutting apple
- kitchen paper
- fabric paint
- saucer for paint
- small sponge paint roller
- plain cotton apron

painted eggs

Real eggs painted in soft pastel colours and tied with sheer organza ribbons make a very simple but effective display for Easter. Older children may like to blow the eggs first, but if smaller children are involved, it is easier simply to boil the eggs before painting and decorating.

1 TAKE THE EGGS Select the eggs and boil the required number for decorating. Allow the eggs to cool completely before you start decorating them. You may like to cut up egg cartons to hold the eggs while you are painting them.

2 PAINT EGGS Paint the eggs in the chosen base colour and allow them to dry completely. You may need to apply a further coat for complete coverage. Allow to dry before adding any further decoration.

3 ADD DECORATION Use a fine paintbrush to add dots, swirls and stripes in a contrasting coloured paint, then allow to dry thoroughly. It is easier to paint one half of the egg first, then to leave it to dry before completing the other side, to prevent the paint from smudging.

4 FINISH OFF Cut lengths of sheer ribbon and tie one around each egg, finishing with a bow. Group the eggs together in a bowl or on a glass cakestand to create a decorative Easter display.

garden tote

Use natural hessian to make this practical yet pretty garden tote, then use it to hold garden tools, seeds, plant labels and other gardening essentials. With its simple but striking painted design of peas and carrots, it would make a great gift for a keen gardener, too.

1 CUT OUT FABRIC Cut a piece of hessian measuring 55cm by 18cm for the main bag, four 10cm by 10cm squares of hessian for the pockets, one oval of hessian (diameter 21cm by 14cm), plus two lengths of hessian measuring 24cm by 8cm for the handles. Use the selvedge of the fabric for the top of the pockets and for one of the longer sides of the handle sections to prevent fraying.

2 DECORATE POCKETS On the remaining three edges of each pocket, carefully pull away strands of hessian to fray the edges about 1cm from each side. Use a brush to paint a design on the pockets. Fix the paint according to the manufacturer's instructions.

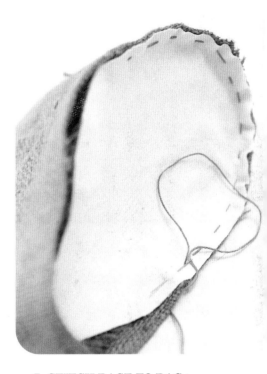

3 ATTACH POCKETS Take the length of the large hessian rectangle (allowing 1cm at each end for seam) and pin the pockets in place at evenly spaced intervals. Using green embroidery thread, make small running stitches to attach the pockets to the bag, leaving the selvedge open at the top.

4 SEW SEAM Fold the piece of hessian with right sides facing, and stitch the sides of the bag together 1cm from the edge. Turn to right side and press both layers of the seam to one side. Using brown embroidery thread, stitch a row of running stitches along this seam to prevent the edges from fraying.

5 STITCH BASE TO BAG Iron the Vilene fabric to one side of the hessian oval (it is advisable for an adult to do this). Now, with right sides facing, stitch the oval to the bag. Whipstitch around the raw edges to prevent any fraying.

6 STITCH TOP HEM Turn the top of the bag 3cm to the inside and press flat with an iron, if necessary. Use lime green embroidery thread and running stitch to secure in place.

7 MAKE HANDLES Lay the two handle sections flat, turn the top and bottom over by 1cm and press. Fold the long edges 2cm to the inside, making sure that the selvedge edge is on top. Use running stitch to hold in place.

8 FINISH OFF The handles should be positioned along the sides of the oval base shape, just above the pockets. Stitch the ends of the handles to the inside of the bag, spacing them approximately 12cm apart. Use whip stitch to hold the handles securely in place.

gingerbread people

Don't just make people – look out for cutters in the shape of a princess, a pony, teddy bear or Santa. Decorate them with chocolate chips, Mini-Smarties® or raisins.

1 Ask an adult to help you preheat the oven to 160°C (325°) Gas 3. Grease several baking trays with soft butter, using a piece of kitchen paper.

2 Set a sieve over a large bowl. Tip the flour, salt and ground ginger into the sieve and sift into the bowl. Add the sugar and mix in with a wooden spoon.

3 Put the butter and syrup into a small saucepan. Ask an adult to help you melt the butter and syrup gently over very low heat – warm the pan just enough to melt the ingredients. Don't let the mixture become hot.

4 Carefully pour the melted mixture into the hollow in the flour.

5 Crack the egg into a small bowl and break up with a fork.

6 Pour the egg into the hollow on top of the melted mixture. Now mix all the ingredients together with a wooden spoon. As soon as the dough starts to come together, put your hands into the bowl and start to push the barely warm dough together. If the dough is too hot to handle, wait for it to cool.

7 As soon as the dough has come together into a ball, and is no longer crumbly, tip it out of the bowl and onto a work surface lightly dusted with flour.

8 With a rolling pin, gently roll out the dough into a large rectangle about 4mm thick.

9 Cut out figures with your cutters, then transfer them carefully to the prepared baking trays with a fish slice or large spatula. Don't worry if their limbs or heads fall off – just press them back together again. Space the figures well apart, because they will spread in the oven. Gather all the trimmings into a ball, then roll out and cut more figures as before.

10 Decorate the figures with raisins, silver balls or Mini-Smarties®. Ask an adult to help you bake the figures – they will take about 15 minutes until golden brown. Watch them carefully, because they can easily burn.

11 Ask an adult to help you carefully remove the trays from the oven and leave them on a heatproof work surface to cool for 5 minutes. This lets the soft biscuit mixture become hard. When the figures are firm, gently lift them onto a wire rack, using a large fish slice or spatula. Let them cool completely.

12 Store in an airtight container and eat within 1 week.

WHAT YOU WILL NEED
- 350g self-raising flour
- a pinch of salt
- 1 tablespoon ground ginger
- 200g caster sugar
- 115g unsalted butter
- 85g golden syrup
- 1 large egg

TO DECORATE
- 2 baking trays
- shaped pastry cutters
- raisins
- edible silver balls
- Mini-Smarties®

makes approximately 14 figures, each 12cm long

pompoms

Old-fashioned pompoms are so easy to make and are a great way of using up left-over wool. They can be made in a variety of sizes and used to create toys, including cute kittens or fluffy chicks for Easter, as well as fun jewellery and decorations.

1 WIND THE WOOL Trace the pompom disc template on page 152 onto paper and cut it out. Place it on a piece of cardboard and draw round it. Repeat. Cut out two discs. Start to wind wool around the two discs. When the first ball of wool is finished, tie the end of the ball to the beginning of a new one. Wind the wool round the disc until it is completely covered.

2 CUT AROUND THE OUTSIDE When the winding process is complete, hold the pompom discs securely in one hand, then cut all around the edges of the wool using scissors. The wool will come away and look like fringing at this point, and it is important that the two discs are firmly held together.

3 SECURE THE WOOL Cut two lengths of wool approximately 20cm long and thread them between the two cardboard discs. Pull together tightly and tie in a knot. It is a good idea to tie several knots so that the wool is very secure.

YOU WILL NEED

⭐ pencil
⭐ scissors
⭐ cardboard for pompom discs
⭐ assorted balls of wool

4 PULL APART AND FINISH

OFF Gently pull away the cardboard discs from the pompom. If it proves difficult to remove them, just cut them off. Trim any excess bits of wool and fluff the pompom ball to give it a nice plump round shape.

cress eggheads

Creating these cute eggheads is really easy and fun. Fill them with cotton wool scattered with fast-growing seed, then sit back and watch the hair grow. Once the cress has sprouted and grown, give the 'hair' a trim and add the yummy sprouts to your lunchtime sandwiches!

1 PREPARE EGGS Remove the top from a hard-boiled egg by gently tapping around the outside of the shell with a knife (make a hole that is large enough for you to extract the egg). Scoop out the egg with a teaspoon.

2 DRAW ON FACE Hold the shell gently in one hand, and draw a face on the outside with a pencil. Don't press too hard, or you might break the shell.

3 ADD COTTON WOOL Gently push a handful of cotton wool into the bottom of the eggshell. Pour in a little water and allow the cotton wool to soak it up.

4 SOW SEED Sow a teaspoonful of seed over the damp cotton wool. Finish off the eggheads by using paint to define the face you drew earlier. Remember to water the cress seeds every day so they do not dry out.

WHAT YOU WILL NEED

✪ hard-boiled eggs
✪ knife
✪ teaspoon
✪ pencil
✪ cotton wool
✪ water
✪ cress or similar seeds

optional: egg carton, lollipop sticks, paint and paintbrush, glue

paper flowers

Paper flowers are easy to make and are a great way of using up scraps of wrapping paper and tissue. Use drinking straws to make stems and stand the flowers in vases made from plastic cups covered in tissue paper. Alternatively, use the flowers to make jewellery or to decorate handmade cards.

1 DRAW OUT FLOWER Trace the flower template on page 153 onto paper and cut out with scissors. Draw around the template on coloured card and cut out the flower shape carefully.

2 CUT OUT PETALS Layer the flowers by cutting out five petals from crêpe or tissue paper in a contrasting colour. These petals can be glued on top of the flower to create a fuller effect.

3 GLUE ON PETALS Fold a small pleat in the bottom end of each petal. Apply glue to the back of a petal and stick it to the centre of the card flower. Repeat for each petal, then let the glue dry completely.

WHAT YOU WILL NEED

✿ paper for flower template
✿ pencil
✿ scissors
✿ coloured card for the main flower shape and the flower centres
✿ coloured tissue paper or crêpe paper
✿ stick of glue
✿ sticky tape
✿ pipe-cleaners for the flower stems

4 FINISH OFF Cut out a small circle of card, approximately 1.5cm in diameter, and glue it to the centre of the flower to cover the ends of the petals. Use a small piece of sticky tape to attach a pipe-cleaner to the back of the flower to form a stem.

tin can windchime

Make a musical windchime using an old tin can and pretty glass beads, then hang it from a tree in the garden. The tin is pierced with small holes for fixing the hanging decorations, so it's important to ask an adult to do this before starting the project.

1 **PIERCE HOLES** Ask an adult to pierce the holes in the tin before you start. You need two holes either side of the open end of the tin for the hanging wire. On the bottom of the tin, pierce one hole in the centre, four holes evenly spaced around the outside edge of the tin, and four holes evenly spaced around the central hole. Now use a fine paintbrush to paint four narrow stripes around the outside of the tin, using the ridges of the tin as an outline.

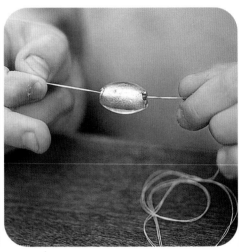

2 **START THREADING** Cut a length of thread approximately 20cm long and then attach one of the metal bells to the bottom, knotting it several times to secure. Begin threading four glass beads onto the string.

3 TIE ON BELLS Repeat until you have made four bead lengths. We used pretty coloured glass beads, but you could use varnished wood beads for a more natural effect.

4 THREAD ON CLAPPER Take a length of thread approximately 20cm long and attach a bell to the end. Knot securely in place. Thread on the metal clapper, so that it hangs from the bottom of the cotton, just above the bell.

5 THREAD ON CHIMES Cut a piece of thread approximately 30cm long. Double it, and knot the ends. Now thread it through the hole in the tubular chime and pull through so that it forms a loop.

6 TIE ON THREAD The tubular chimes, clapper and beaded decorations are all attached to the inside of the tin by feeding the thread through the holes in the tin base and pulling through. The clapper must go through the central hole in the bottom of the tin and the tubular chimes around this. Finally, thread the beaded decorations through the outside holes.

7 FIX WIRE HANDLE Thread a 30cm length of fine wire through the two holes punched in the sides of the top (open) end of the tin. Twist the wire around itself to secure in place. This is the loop from which to hang your windchime.

8 FINISH OFF Gather all the pieces of thread together, push the ends through a bead, and knot securely. The bead will prevent the pieces of thread slipping through the hole in the base.

papier mâché dinosaur

Papier mâché is a really hands-on messy project, so make sure you have enough time to get the materials ready and to clear up afterwards! Kids love working with papier mâché due to its sloshy consistency and the fact it can be used to create fantastic three-dimensional objects.

WHAT YOU WILL NEED
- ✪ newspaper
- ✪ balloon
- ✪ bowl to support balloon
- ✪ thick brushes
- ✪ PVA glue
- ✪ bowl for glue
- ✪ kitchen foil (for the dinosaur's legs and head)
- ✪ masking tape
- ✪ cardboard
- ✪ two different colours of paint

1 COVER BALLOON Tear the newspaper into strips and put to one side. Blow up the balloon and balance it on a bowl while you stick on the paper. Using a brush, apply glue all over the balloon. Cover with strips of newspaper. Repeat the process, building up layers of paper, until the balloon is thickly covered.

2 ADD LEGS AND HEAD We used ordinary kitchen foil rolled into short cylinder shapes to make the legs and head. Use masking tape to attach them to the balloon. Now apply a coat of glue to the legs and head and cover with strips of paper. Make sure that the strips overlap onto the body, so that the head and legs will be securely held in place once the glue has dried.

3 ADD SPINES Cut out triangles measuring approximately 2.5cm/1in wide and 4cm/1oin high from the cardboard. Fold the bottom of the triangle at a ninety-degree angle and glue the flat part to the balloon. Form two lines to create the spines. When the glue is dry, apply another layer of paper to hold the spikes in place.

4 FINISH OFF It is best to leave the papier mâché overnight to make sure all the layers are completely dry. Paint the dinosaur body in mauve and the spikes in bright blue. Allow the paint to dry. We added some more blue spots to the body to finish off.

wooden nesting box

Plain wooden nesting boxes can be decorated with lollipop sticks and painted in soft pastel colours to create these fun boxes that will make a pretty addition to any tree or wall in the garden. Hang it in a sheltered spot, at least 2m above the ground.

1 APPLY UNDERCOAT Use a large paintbrush to apply undercoat to the nesting box. Let it dry completely. Apply a second coat if necessary.

2 PAINT BASE COLOUR Once the undercoat is dry, use a brush to apply the first coat of green paint to the nesting box. Do not paint over the undercoat on the roof, however. Apply a further coat of paint, if required, and allow to dry thoroughly.

3 PAINT CRAFT STICKS Apply undercoat to one side and the edges of the standard-sized craft sticks, then leave them to dry. Next, paint the other sides of the sticks and leave them to dry. Once completely dry, paint the sticks cream.

4 PAINT STICKS FOR ROOF Now take the larger craft sticks and divide them into two piles. Paint one pile of the larger craft sticks green, and the other ones cream. Allow to dry completely. Apply a further coat, if required.

5 GLUE ON ROOF Use strong glue to fix the large craft sticks to the roof. Glue them in alternate colours to create a striped effect, then leave the glue to dry.

6 ATTACH PICKET FENCE Ask an adult to cut four of the smaller craft sticks in half to create the picket fence. Line them up along the base of the front of the nesting box and glue them in an even row along this edge.

7 FINISH OFF Position the remaining two smaller craft sticks horizontally across the top and bottom of the row of craft sticks then glue in place. Finish the nesting box with one or two coats of varnish to make it suitable for outdoor use.

summer

funky fans

Create fans using brightly coloured and decorative paper – sheets of wrapping paper are a perfect choice. Finished off with silk tassels, paper fans are easy to make, and are a great addition to the dressing-up box.

1 CUT OUT To make a paper fan, cut out one piece of paper measuring approximately 50cm x 25cm. The paper should not be too thin, or the finished fan will be floppy.

2 FOLD PAPER Place the sheet of paper flat on the table with the shortest edge in front of you. Starting at the end closest to you, make even folds that are approximately 2cm wide, turning the paper over each time for a pleated effect. Press each fold flat (you could use a ruler to rub over the fold to make it as flat as possible).

3 DECORATE To decorate the fan, open out the pleats slightly and use glue to create a swirling pattern along the top edge of the paper. Scatter glitter over the glue and shake to remove the excess. Allow the glue to dry before folding up the fan again.

4 FINISH OFF Pinch the pleats at the bottom of the fan together, and insert the end of the silk tassel in between the central pleats. Use a stapler to secure the pleats (two or three staples are usually sufficient). If children are very young, an adult should be responsible for the stapling.

pressing flowers

The traditional art of flower pressing will delight young children and the finished items can be used to decorate all manner of objects. We used a flower press, but leaves and flowers can be easily pressed between the pages of a heavy book or telephone directory and left for a few days to dry out.

1 CHOOSE FLOWERS It is fun to pick the flowers from the garden, but if this is not possible use shop-bought flowers. The flatter the flower, the easier it will be to press. If the flower is bulky, pull off the petals, press them individually and use them to recreate the flower once they are pressed.

2 PRESS FLOWERS Carefully place the flowers and leaves in the press between the layers of paper and card. Replace the top of the flower press and tighten the screws as firmly as you can. This ensures that as little air as possible can get to the flowers and leaves. An adult may need to help tighten the screws.

3 REMOVE FLOWERS The flowers and leaves should be left in the press for about a week until they are completely dry. Once they are dry, peel them away from the papers in the press as carefully as possible, as they become fragile once dry. Place them on a sheet of paper ready for application.

WHAT YOU WILL NEED

- flowers and leaves
- flower press
- object for decoration (e.g. bookmark, picture frame or greetings card)
- glue
- brushes for glue
- tweezers for lifting flowers, if required

4 APPLY TO DESIRED OBJECT

Apply a thin layer of glue to the back of a flower. Gently lift the flower and place it in the required position (use tweezers if necessary). Add other flowers until the design is complete. Allow to dry thoroughly. If decorating a box, apply a layer of water-based acrylic varnish.

painted pots

These terracotta plant pots have been painted in fun bright shades then decorated with bold contrasting spots. Plant them up with cheerful annuals and display them indoors or out, or give them as gifts to friends and relatives.

WHAT YOU WILL NEED

- ✪ terracotta plant pots
- ✪ saucer for paint
- ✪ assorted paintbrushes
- ✪ undercoat
- ✪ coloured paint
- ✪ pencil
- ✪ water-based acrylic varnish

1 CHOOSE MATERIALS Apply undercoat to the pots and allow them to dry thoroughly. Paint the inside of the pot with the undercoat to about halfway down, so that the terracotta does not show. Apply a further coat if required.

2 PAINT BASE COLOUR Now apply a coat of the base colour to the outside and inside of the pot, and allow it to dry completely. For more even coverage, apply a further coat of paint and allow to dry.

3 FINISH OFF Use a pencil to carefully draw the spots on the outside of the pot. Apply the contrasting paint, using a fine brush to fill in the spots, and allow to dry. Finish the pot with a coat of hard-wearing water-based acrylic varnish.

modelling with balsa wood

Lightweight balsa wood is easy to cut and glue, which makes it ideal for children to use for modelling. Small pieces can be cut with scissors, but thicker pieces of balsa should be cut by an adult using a junior hacksaw.

1 GLUE BASE Cut seven lengths of balsa wood measuring 10cm x 1cm x 1cm for the base of the boat. Lay two pieces of the wood about 9cm apart and glue the other five pieces on the top at equal intervals. For the mast, cut two squares of wood measuring 1cm x 1cm and two lengths measuring 10cm x 5mm.

2 PAINT BASE Now paint the base of the boat and the mast sections and allow them to dry completely. You may need to apply a further coat of paint to ensure even coverage. Allow the paint to dry completely before attaching the mast.

3 MAKE SAIL AND MAST Cut out a triangle of fabric about 8cm high and 8cm wide, using pinking shears to prevent the fabric from fraying. Lay one mast piece on the table and apply glue down the centre of the fabric triangle before placing it on top. Lay the second mast on top, so the sail is sandwiched between the pieces of wood, then glue in place. Allow to dry.

4 ATTACH SAIL Glue the base of the mast to the two squares of balsa wood so that it is held between them. Apply a blob of glue to the centre of the boat base, and stick the sail and mast to the base. Allow the glue to dry. You may wish to apply more paint to cover the glue in this area.

WHAT YOU WILL NEED

✪ balsa wood in assorted lengths and thicknesses (most craft or modelling shops sell packs of balsa wood)
✪ scissors or junior hacksaw
✪ glue
✪ paint
✪ paintbrushes in various sizes
✪ saucers to hold paint
✪ scraps of fabric for sail
✪ pinking shears

herb planter

Growing herbs is a great way to learn about edible plants, and they're a doddle to grow in a window box on a sunny window ledge or patio. For a never-ending supply of tasty leaves, all you need to do is keep on picking them!

1 COVER HOLES Before filling your window box with compost, cover the drainage holes in the base. Use large stones or pieces of broken terracotta pot. This will allow water to drain away, but prevent the holes from getting clogged with compost. It will also prevent compost spilling through the holes and onto surfaces.

2 ADD COMPOST Cover the base of the container with a 1cm-deep layer of compost, breaking any large clods apart with your hands. Roughly level the compost with your fingers to leave a smooth finish.

3 ARRANGE PLANTS Take your plants out of their containers and arrange them in the window box. Upright plants will look better in the centre of the container, while creeping plants are best tumbling over the ends. Once you are happy with your display, fill the gaps around the plants with compost, leaving a level surface about 2cm below the top of the trough. Firm around the plants with your fingertips and water them well.

WHAT YOU WILL NEED

✿ large terracotta window box
✿ stones or large pieces of broken terracotta
✿ John Innes 3 compost
✿ small trowel
✿ selection of herbs to fill your trough (we used chives, rosemary, mint, oregano and thyme)
✿ watering can

harvesting herbs

During late spring and summer, herbs make lots of fresh new growth, which is perfect for harvesting and drying. Store dried herbs in cellophane bags, and keep them handy in the kitchen. They also make great presents to give to friends.

WHAT YOU WILL NEED
- herbs to cut
- scissors
- bowl
- paper towels
- tray
- greaseproof paper
- small cellophane bags
- labels

1 CUT HERBS Select a handful of fresh, healthy new shoots and snip them off with a pair of scissors. To ensure the parent plant is left in good shape, cut just above a pair of leaves. Fill a bowl with cold water and quickly dip the shoots to remove any dirt, then gently dry them on paper towels.

2 PREPARE TO DRY Cover a tray with a sheet of greaseproof paper and lay the shoots on top to dry. If you are drying different kinds of herbs, make sure they are not touching. Now put the tray in an airing cupboard until the herbs have dried completely.

3 FINISH OFF Carefully remove the individual leaves and put them into small cellophane bags. Fold over and secure the top of the bag to keep the contents fresh. Add a label, then store the herbs in a kitchen cupboard.

tie-dye t-shirt

Tie-dyeing is a simple process with striking results. You can give old white T-shirts a new lease of life with this technique, but it is is advisable to have an adult on hand, as it can get quite messy. Alternatively, follow the steps shown here to create the design, but use machine dye rather than the bucket method, as it's an easier (and less messy) option.

1 TIE UP MATERIAL Tie the string around the sleeves of the T-shirt in two places and pull tightly to ensure no dye can get through. Repeat on the body of the T-shirt, tying two pieces of string at 10cm intervals. If you want additional stripes, tie more lengths of string around the T-shirt.

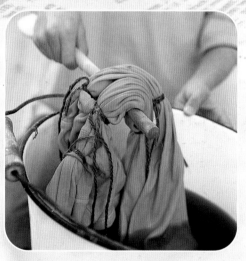

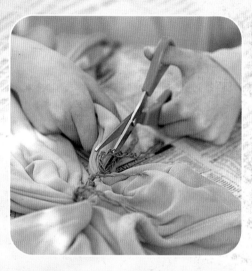

2 PLACE ITEM IN DYE

Following the manufacturer's instructions, make up the dye in a bucket, adding dye fix if necessary. Push the T-shirt into the bucket of dye and stir gently with a wooden spoon to ensure the fabric is evenly covered with the dye. Leave the T-shirt for approximately one hour, stirring occasionally.

3 REMOVE THE T-SHIRT

When the dye process is complete, carefully remove the T-shirt from the bucket and wash the items according to the dye manufacturer's instructions. Leave the strings in place on the T-shirt.

4 CUT THE STRINGS

Allow the T-shirt to dry completely. Now use a pair of scissors to carefully cut the strings, taking care not to damage the T-shirt. Ask an adult to help iron the T-shirt to remove the crease marks left by the string.

crystallised pansies

Real pansies make the daintiest of decorations for a plate of cute cupcakes, and they even taste good too! Egg white and caster sugar is all that you need to create these pretty crystallised flowers.

1 PAINT ON EGG WHITE
Using a fine paintbrush, paint each flower with egg white. Paint no more than five or six flowers at a time, as the egg white tends to dry quite quickly.

2 SPRINKLE ON SUGAR Use a spoon to gently sprinkle caster sugar over the flowers, making sure not to add too much sugar. Leave to dry. The flowers will become hard and brittle.

3 FINISH OFF Use two or three of the crystallised flowers to decorate each cupcake. Serve on a pretty cake plate or glass cakestand.

WHAT YOU WILL NEED

- ✪ plate
- ✪ paintbrush
- ✪ whites of 2 eggs
- ✪ fresh pansies
- ✪ spoon
- ✪ caster sugar
- ✪ cupcakes
- ✪ cake plate or cakestand

split-pin animals

Split-pin animals are fun to make and educational, too, as they teach young children about joints and movement. As you cut out and make the animals, describe how the sections will move when held together by the split pins. The pins can also be used decoratively, to make buttons and eyes for the creatures.

1 **CUT OUT** Trace the teddy templates on page 153 onto plain paper and cut them out. Draw around the templates on a piece of card and cut them out. You will need twelve identical-sized ovals for the teddy's legs, arms and ears, then one each for the nose, head and body. We used different-coloured card for the teddy's nose.

2 **GLUE ON NOSE** Use glue to stick the nose to the teddy's face and allow it to dry completely. Lay out all the pieces of the teddy bear on a table so you can work out where the positions for the holes should be.

3 **MARK AND CUT HOLES** Use a pencil to mark the holes for the pins, making sure that each of the card sections overlap at this point, so they will be held together by the pins. Use a sharp blade to make slits through the layers of card. It is advisable for an adult to do this, as sharp blades are dangerous.

4 **INSERT THE SPLIT PINS** Insert the split pins through each slit and fold them flat at the back of the bear. Continue until the whole teddy has been assembled. We added a decorative pin through the teddy's nose as a finishing touch.

colourful annuals

Annuals will fill your garden with cheerful colour. Buy them as plants in early summer and they will flower non-stop through until autumn. For a really fun, jazzy display, use your imagination and plant them in the most unusual containers you can find.

3 FINISH OFF Use more compost to fill any gaps around the edges of the rootball and firm down with your fingertips. Water the plants, but don't overdo it, as the beaker doesn't have any drainage holes. Add some water, allow it to soak in, then test by pushing your finger into the compost. If it's thoroughly wet, you don't need to add any more.

2 PLANT UP Sit a plant on top of the compost. The surface of the rootball needs to be just beneath the lip of the pot, so add or remove compost as necessary.

1 ADD COMPOST Put a handful of compost in the bottom of a beaker. Don't worry about drainage holes, as annual plants only last for a short time.

father's day gift

These decorative keyrings are made from balsa wood and thin wood sheets, and make the perfect gift for Father's Day. Key chains are available from craft shops and are easily attached to the wood. Both boys and girls will enjoy this easy woodwork technique.

1 CUT SIMPLE SHAPES Cut small rectangles from the wood sheet. This will be the base of the keyring. Now draw simple motifs straight onto the balsa wood and cut them out using scissors. An adult may need to assist a younger child in cutting the wood.

2 PAINT BASE AND CUTOUTS Paint the base of the keyring all over the back and front and allow to dry. A further coat of paint may be necessary for even coverage. Paint the front and edges of the smaller balsa-wood pieces using a fine paintbrush. Allow to dry.

3 GLUE ON MOTIF Apply glue to the back of the balsa-wood pieces and stick them in place on the front of the keyring. Press down firmly. Allow the glue to dry completely. You may wish to apply a coat of water-based acrylic varnish to make the keyring more hard-wearing.

4 ATTACH CHAIN Make a small hole at the top of the keyring using a bradawl. For safety reasons, it is advisable for an adult to do this part of the project. Take the keyring attachment, thread the metal loop through the hole, and close using pliers.

pretty plant labels

Jumbo craft sticks with butterfly-shaped ends make pretty plant markers that identify plants growing in pots or the garden. Paint them in strong pastel shades that will stand out against the lush green of foliage, and write on the name of the plant in pencil.

WHAT YOU WILL NEED
- paint
- small paintbrushes
- natural wood jumbo craft sticks
- undercoat
- pencil

1 APPLY UNDERCOAT
Use a small paintbrush to apply a coat of undercoat to the craft stick. Let it dry completely and add a second coat if the coverage is patchy.

2 PAINT MARKERS
When the undercoat is completely dry, apply paint in your chosen colour to one side and the edges of a craft stick, and leave it to dry. Next, paint the other side of the stick and, again, leave it to dry. Apply a further coat, if required.

3 WRITE ON PLANT NAMES
Once the painted markers are completely dry, write on the plant names. There is usually a tag or sticky label on the pot that a plant comes in (or on a seed packet, if you have grown it from seed). Copy this in clear, bold writing. Now the marker is ready to be pushed into the earth alongside the plant that it identifies.

autumn

peanut heart

Peanuts can be easily pierced and threaded onto wire to fun-shaped bird feeders that our feathered friends will appreciate during the winter months. We finished off this heart-shaped feeder with a raffia bow to create a pretty and practical garden ornament.

WHAT YOU WILL NEED
- ✪ peanuts
- ✪ wooden skewer or bradawl for piercing holes
- ✪ strong wire
- ✪ raffia for bow
- ✪ twine for hanging loop (approximately 20cm)

1 PIERCE HOLES IN PEANUTS
Ask an adult to pierce the holes in the nuts using a wooden skewer or a bradawl. You will need approximately 60 peanuts to make one peanut heart.

2 THREAD PEANUTS Fold the wire in half to create the 'V' shape of the heart. Begin threading peanuts onto the wire. Each side needs around 30 peanuts.

3 FINISH OFF Ask an adult to bend each side of the heart into a curve to form a heart shape and twist the wire to fix the ends in place. Now tie a raffia bow at the top of the heart to cover the wire ends. Cut a 20cm length of twine to form the hanging loop, and suspend your bird feeder from a branch in the garden.

covering books

Use pretty handmade paper to cover textbooks or notebooks. You can use them at school or give them as gifts. The same technique can be used to decorate boxes or photo albums, which make welcome keepsakes.

1 CUT OUT PAPER Lay the book flat on the piece of decorative paper. Cut all around the book, leaving a margin of about 4cm of extra paper around the sides. Where the spine of the book lies, cut two slits in the paper at the top and bottom of the book, and neatly fold them inwards to hide them.

3 CUT OUT DECORATIONS Use scissors to cut out flowers, petals and whatever other decorations are desired. These can be drawn using a pencil first, or cut out freehand, depending on the child.

2 GLUE ON COVER Fold the remaining edges of the paper towards the inside of the book and make pleated folds at the corners to neaten the edges. Glue the paper in place and allow to dry completely. It is a good idea to glue each layer of paper at the folded corners so they stay in place.

4 DECORATE Lay out the paper shapes on the book to create the design. When you are happy with your arrangement, glue each piece in place. If the pieces are small, use a fine paintbrush to apply the glue to the back of the paper. Allow to dry thoroughly.

indoor garden

You don't need to have a garden to grow plants. Small houseplants can be planted together in large glass jars to create an eye-catching display that needs very little watering or care. These gardens in a bottle look great when placed on a windowsill or shelf.

1 ADD CLAY PELLETS Make sure the inside of the glass container is clean (so you can see the plants!) then slowly pour in your clay pellets to make a 5cm drainage layer in the base of the jar.

2 POUR IN CHARCOAL Damp compost can become smelly, so pour a thin layer of horticultural charcoal over the clay pellets, to keep it fresh.

3 FILL WITH COMPOST Fill a quarter of the container with compost and press it down with your fingers (if your wrist can't fit freely through the neck of the bottle, use the back of a long-handled spoon to press the compost down).

4 PLANT UP JAR Use the long-handled spoon to excavate small planting holes and lower plants into position. Firm the compost around the rootballs with the spoon. When you have finished planting, drop in some more clay pellets to cover any bare patches.

5 WATER PLANTS Water the compost until it's saturated. If you leave the lid open you'll have to water regularly, but if you close it the humidity inside the jar should provide enough moisture for the plants.

WHAT YOU WILL NEED

- ✪ glass container (we used a Kilner jar)
- ✪ clay pellets
- ✪ horticultural charcoal
- ✪ multi-purpose compost
- ✪ long-handled spoon, if necessary
- ✪ a selection of plants (enough to fill your container)
- ✪ watering can

harvest wreath

Decorate a ready-made wreath with your own dried leaves to create a decorative harvest wreath to hang on the wall or front door. Collect a variety of attractive, different-coloured leaves in autumn and use a flower press or large book to press them flat.

1 COLLECT AND DRY LEAVES Collect leaves for drying, making sure they are not damp. Place them between layers of paper in a thick book or flower press and leave for two or three weeks until dry. Put a dab of glue on the back of each leaf, and attach to the heart wreath.

2 GLUE ON LEAVES Continue to glue leaves to the wreath and add sycamore wings and dried seedheads at regular intervals. Allow the glue to dry completely.

3 FINISH OFF Thread the gingham ribbon through the top of the heart wreath. Knot the ends, and you will have a hanging loop that you can suspend the wreath from.

cat mask

This fun cat mask is perfect for Halloween or a fancy-dress party. Black is the best choice for Halloween, but it would look equally cute in brown or white. Add some pipe-cleaner whiskers and a little pompom for the cat's nose.

1 DRAW TEMPLATES Trace the mask template on page 154 onto a piece of folded card and cut it out. Open out the template. Take the piece of black felt and glue it to the piece of black card. Allow to dry.

2 CUT OUT MASK Draw around the paper template on the card side of the glued card and felt. Carefully cut out with scissors, taking particular care when cutting out the eye holes. An adult may need to help by first making a slit in the card for the eyes, so that the scissors can be easily inserted for cutting.

3 ATTACH NOSE AND WHISKERS Glue the pompom nose onto the mask. Cut six pipe-cleaner whiskers measuring approximately 10cm in length, and glue them to each side of the mask, just below the eye holes. Allow to dry.

4 ATTACH ELASTIC BAND Using a hole punch, make a hole on each side of the mask in the position indicated on the template. Thread one end of the elastic through the hole and knot to secure. Thread the elastic through the other hole, knot, and trim any excess elastic to finish.

mirror-image painting

This is a perfect project for toddlers, who will be fascinated by the process. You may have to do the painting in stages – for example, the lion's face first, then the mane – otherwise the paint dries too quickly.

1 **FOLD PAPER IN HALF** Fold the paper in half, pressing down flat to form a crease. Open up the paper and draw a semicircle on one side of the paper in pencil (you may like to use a plate to draw a more accurate circle).

2 **START PAINTING** Fill in the semicircle with paint. It is important to do this fairly quickly, or the paint will start to dry and will not transfer properly to the other side of the paper when it is folded.

3 **FOLD OVER** Fold the paper in half on the original crease and press down firmly. Open the paper to reveal the mirror image of the face. The next stage is the lion's mane – again, it may be easier to draw this before painting. Fill in the triangles with paint, fold the paper in half, and open up to reveal the mane.

4 FINISH OFF Fill in one eye and half of the mouth using brown paint. Fold the paper in half, press it flat and open to reveal the lion's face. As a finishing touch, we added a pompom for the lion's nose.

halloween hat

A simple cone shape in black card is the basis of this spooky witch's hat with a brim, or the simpler wizard's hat without a brim. Decorate with black net and silver stars for a night of trick-or-treating!

1 MEASURE AND CUT Cut out a semicircle of black card with a diameter of approximately 60cm. Roll into a cone shape and fit to the child's head. Mark out the line where the card should be joined. Use strong tape to create the cone (we used black plumber's tape, which is the same colour as the hat). A couple of staples will make the hat more secure.

2 CUT OUT BRIM Place the cone on a sheet of black card and draw all the way around the opening. Then draw another larger circle approximately 8cm wider, to form the brim. Mark out a smaller circle 2cm within the inner circle to allow for the flaps for the brim. Cut out the brim from the card. Use scissors to cut the flaps for the brim at intervals of 2cm all the way around the inner circle.

3 ATTACH HAT AND BRIM Fold alternate flaps back and sit the cone on top of the brim. Use sticky tape to fix the flaps to the cone. Firmly press down the tape to keep the brim in place.

4 DECORATE We used a star-shaped cookie cutter as a template to draw stars on silver paper. Cut them out with scissors and glue carefully to the hat. We also added a length of black netting, which we glued to the point of the hat as a finishing touch.

seed necklace

When it's too cold or wet to play outside, why not make your own jewellery from dried pumpkin seeds and sycamore wings threaded on cotton? It's a great way of using up the seeds from the carved Halloween pumpkin project on pages 104–105.

1 WASH THEM Put all the seeds in a bowl of warm water and leave to soak for a couple of hours so that the flesh comes away from the seeds. Carefully pick out the seeds and place in a colander.

2 RINSE SEEDS When all the seeds are in the colander, run them under a tap to remove any bits of pumpkin flesh.

3 DRY AND PIERCE SEEDS Lay the seeds in rows on a tray covered with a clean tea towel. Leave in a warm, dry place until the seeds have dried out. This can take up to a week. When the seeds are dry, use a needle to pierce holes through each seed ready for threading onto the necklace. It is advisable for an adult to carry out this task for younger children.

4 THREAD ON SEEDS Thread the cotton thread on the needle and knot the ends. Begin threading the seeds and intersperse them with sycamore wings. When threading is complete, tie the ends of the thread in a knot to finish.

WHAT YOU WILL NEED

- ✪ spoon
- ✪ pumpkin seeds
- ✪ bowl of warm water
- ✪ colander
- ✪ tray
- ✪ tea towel
- ✪ needle for making holes
- ✪ cotton thread
- ✪ sycamore wings

pretty seed packets

It's fun and satisfying harvesting your own seeds and then packaging them up for the following year in these pretty decorated envelopes. You could also give them to family and friends.

1 DECORATE ENVELOPE
Using coloured pencils, decorate the edges of the front of the envelope with pretty designs, such as wavy lines and and tiny polka dots.

2 DRAW ON DESIGN Now draw the shape of a flower or vegetable, depending on what sort of seeds are in the envelope, using the coloured pencils. You could add the name of the seeds in your best handwriting.

3 PUNCH HOLES Use a hole punch to make two holes at the top of the envelope, just where the flap is situated. Now carefully put the seeds in the envelope, and seal it closed.

WHAT YOU WILL NEED

- ✪ small brown envelopes
- ✪ coloured pencils
- ✪ hole punch
- ✪ seeds
- ✪ 25cm raffia ribbon per packet
- ✪ scissors

4 FINISH OFF Thread the raffia through the two punched holes and tie in a decorative bow. Trim the ends of the raffia with scissors to finish.

lavender bags

These simple but very pretty lavender bags are easy to sew and make lovely gifts for family and friends. We used a combination of a pastel-coloured floral print and spotty cotton fabric to create these vintage-style lavender bags.

1 CUT AND DRY LAVENDER
Using scissors, carefully snip off long stems of lavender. Cover a tray with a sheet of greaseproof or waxed paper and place the lavender on top to dry. Put the tray in an airing cupboard until the herbs have dried completely. When dry, carefully pull off the lavender heads by hand and collect them in a bowl ready to fill your bags.

2 CUT OUT THE BAGS Using pinking shears to prevent the fabric edges from fraying, cut out a rectangle of fabric measuring 12 x 40cm, or two rectangles measuring 12 x 20cm.

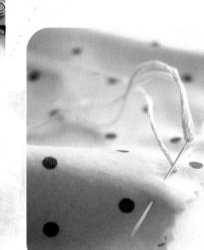

3 STITCH BAGS With wrong sides facing, stitch together the sides of the fabric and base of bag using running stitch and contrasting coloured cotton embroidery thread. The stitches should be no more than 1cm apart, so the lavender does not leak out.

4 FILL WITH LAVENDER
When the bag is complete, use a teaspoon to carefully fill it with loose lavender. Fill the bag to approximately halfway up, and make sure it is quite plump and full.

5 FINISH OFF Lay the lavender bag on one side and wrap the cotton ribbon around the bag, just above the lavender. Tie a bow, then trim the ends using scissors.

WHAT YOU WILL NEED
- ✿ scissors
- ✿ greaseproof paper
- ✿ tray
- ✿ dried lavender heads
- ✿ pinking shears
- ✿ floral fabric (each bag uses two rectangles fabric approximately 12 x 20cm or a single rectangle 12 x 40cm)
- ✿ cotton embroidery thread
- ✿ needle
- ✿ 25cm narrow white ribbon per bag

pumpkin lantern

This carved Halloween pumpkin looks more friendly than spooky! He's been given a pointy parsnip nose and a thick head of carrot-frond 'hair'. Fill him with tealights and leave him by the door to greet trick-or-treaters.

1 SCOOP OUT SEEDS Ask an adult to cut the top off the pumpkin using a sharp knife. Scoop out the flesh and seeds using an ice-cream scoop or a large spoon.

2 DRAW ON FACE Draw eyes, nose and a mouth onto the pumpkin using a felt-tip pen. Ask an adult to cut out the shapes using a sharp knife.

3 INSERT NOSE Push the thick end of the parsnip into the nose hole to make a pointy nose. Cut the fronds from the carrots to prepare the hair.

4 FINISH OFF Lay the carrot fronds around the top of the pumpkin to make the hair. Place two or three tealights inside the pumpkin and ask an adult to light them. Now place the pumpkin by the front door.

winter

twig decorations

These delicate-looking star decorations are crafted from thin twigs gathered from the garden or the park, painted silver and then tied together with fine wire. The twig stars look so pretty dangling in a row from a mantelpiece or hung in clusters on a Christmas tree.

1 APPLY PAINT Choose three 10cm-long twigs and paint them silver. Allow to dry thoroughly. If required, apply a second coat of paint for more even coverage and leave to dry.

2 FORM STAR SHAPE Lay the three twigs one on top of each other to form a star shape. Cut a length of fine wire and bind it round the twigs to hold the star in place. Wrap the wire over the twigs several times, so that they are completely secure.

3 ATTACH HANGING LOOP Cut a length of thread for the hanging loop and fold it in half. Wrap it round one 'arm' of the star, thread the ends back through the loop, and pull to attach the thread to the twig. Knot the two loose ends together to form a hanging loop.

WHAT YOU WILL NEED
- ✪ thin twigs
- ✪ silver paint
- ✪ fine paintbrush
- ✪ fine wire for tying
- ✪ scissors
- ✪ silver cotton or nylon thread for hanging loops

orange tree decorations

Dried orange slices hung from a pretty gingham ribbon loop make fragrant and unusual Christmas tree decorations. They also make a great addition to our pot pourri, which can be found on pages 124-125.

1 SLICE THE ORANGES Ask an adult to cut the orange into slices that are approximately 5mm wide. Now put the slices on a tea towel and gently blot them with kitchen towel to remove any excess moisture. This should speed up the drying process.

2 BAKE IN OVEN Lay the orange slices on a metal baking tray. Put them in the oven on the very lowest setting and leave them for about four hours or until they are completely dry. The trick is to let them 'cook' long enough to dry completely. If the orange slices do not dry entirely, they won't keep for long and may even go mouldy. Ask an adult to remove the tray from the oven, as it will be very hot.

3 REMOVE DRIED ORANGES Once the tray has completely cooled, remove the orange slices from the tray and set them aside for decorating. The slices should be hard and dry, but retain their delicious citrussy fragrance.

WHAT YOU WILL NEED

- ✪ fresh oranges
- ✪ sharp knife
- ✪ tea towel
- ✪ kitchen towel
- ✪ baking tray
- ✪ wooden skewer or awl
- ✪ 15cm gingham ribbon (10mm wide)
  for each hanging loop

4 FINISH OFF Ask an adult to make a small hole in the orange using a sharp point such as a wooden skewer. Thread the ribbon through the hole and tie the ends in a knot. Trim the ribbon ends on the diagonal to prevent them from fraying.

paper chains

Traditional paper chains are so easy to make, and look fantastic at children's parties or other celebrations. We used a combination of zingy hot pinks and oranges, but you could try making paper chains in soft pastel tones or in red and white to use as Christmas decorations.

1 CHOOSE COLOURS Ask your child what colours she or he would like to use to create the chains. For more decorative paper chains, you could use patterned wrapping paper or translucent tracing paper, which is available from art shops in a variety of different colours.

2 DRAW STRIPS Using a pencil and ruler, draw the strips on the back of the paper, making sure that each one is approximately 2cm wide. An A4-sized sheet of paper, used landscape, should give around fourteen strips.

3 CUT STRIPS Using scissors, cut out the strips. It is a good idea to keep the colours separate by making a pile of strips in each colour, so they are easier to select when joining the chains together.

4 GLUE STRIPS INTO CHAINS Form a loop with the first paper chain and put a dab of glue on one end to stick it together. For the next link, thread the paper through the loop and glue the ends. Repeat to make more links, until you have made the required length of paper chain.

WHAT YOU WILL NEED

✪ selection of coloured paper at least
28cm wide
✪ pencil
✪ ruler
✪ scissors
✪ glue
✪ brush for glue

4
the
the
als
pla
ov
ins
hav

felt motif cards

Felt is great for decorating cards as it comes in a wide selection of colours and does not fray once it is cut. We used Christmas-themed cookie cutters as templates for a variety of festive designs. Glue the felt shapes onto cardboard and finish them with dainty ribbon bows.

1 CUT OUT FELT MOTIF Use the circular cookie cutter (or a similar object) as a template for the round shape on this card. Place it on the felt and draw aound it with a pencil. Carefully cut out the round shape. If you are making more than one card, it's a good idea to cut out all your felt shapes at the same time.

2 GLUE ON HANGING LOOP Cut a piece of gingham ribbon about 5cm long and fold it into a loop. Glue the ribbon onto the card. Press down firmly to fix it in place.

3 STICK ON FELT SHAPE Apply a thin layer of glue to the back of the felt shape and stick it onto the card, making sure that you have concealed the ends of the ribbon loop. Press down firmly and allow to dry completely.

4 FINISHING Make a ribbon bow from the gingham ribbon. Apply a tiny dab of glue to the back of the bow, and stick to the front of the felt motif. Press down firmly to secure it in place and leave to dry.

1 PAI
saucers
small a
colours
to apply
hand. M
too thic
in case

WHAT YOU WILL NEED
- ✪ round cookie cutter
- ✪ felt squares
- ✪ pencil
- ✪ scissors
- ✪ 15cm gingham ribbon, 6mm wide
- ✪ glue
- ✪ blank cards

peppermint creams

Delicious to eat and oh-so-easy to make, peppermint creams make great gifts and the mixture can be used to form fun shapes, such as these cute snowmen with their black icing hats and snug blue scarves!

1 MIX INGREDIENTS Sift the icing sugar into a bowl and stir in the condensed milk until the mixture becomes a smooth paste. Add three drops of oil of peppermint and knead it into the mixture until the flavour is thoroughly worked through. Add more oil of peppermint a drop at a time and knead it in thoroughly until you achieve the desired intensity of flavour.

2 FORM SNOWMEN Roll the mixture between the palms of your hands to form a ball for the bottom half of the snowman. Place in a petit-four case, then roll a smaller ball for the head. Place the head gently on top of the larger ball and push down gently so the balls stick to each other.

3 ADD SCARVES Roll out the pale blue icing. Ask an adult to use a sharp knife to cut lengths measuring about 3mm wide by 10cm long. Wrap one around the neck of each snowman to form a scarf.

4 FINISH OFF Use ready-mixed black icing to form the snowmen's hats and eyes. To finish, roll blobs of brown icing into tiny balls for the snowmen's noses and stick them firmly in place. Let the snowmen dry completely before packaging them up.

WHAT YOU WILL NEED
- ✪ 500g icing sugar
- ✪ 4 tablespoons condensed milk
- ✪ oil of peppermint
- ✪ miniature silver petit-four cases
- ✪ pale blue ready-rolled icing
- ✪ ready-mixed tubes of black and brown icing

makes 16 snowmen

WHAT YOU WILL NEED

- ✪ pine cones, cinnamon sticks and dried orange slices (see pages 110–111)
- ✪ cellophane bags
- ✪ air-drying clay
- ✪ small heart-shaped cookie cutter
- ✪ drinking straw
- ✪ green paint
- ✪ paintbrush
- ✪ 20cm narrow gingham ribbon (10mm wide)
- ✪ 30cm gingham ribbon (20mm wide)

pot pourri

Sweetly scented pot pourri is fun and easy to make and is always a welcome gift. It looks very pretty packaged in a glossy cellophane bag and decorated with ribbon and little heart-shaped clay decorations.

1 FILL BAG Make the dried orange slices following the instructions on pages 110–111. Put the cones, cinnamon sticks and orange slices into a bowl. Now fill the cellophane bag with the pot pourri, layering the different items for an attractive effect.

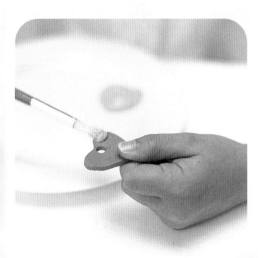

2 PAINT CLAY DECORATIONS Following the instructions on pages 86–87, make two clay hearts per bag of pot pourri. Use a heart-shaped cookie cutter to cut them out, and use a drinking straw to pierce a hole in each one to thread the ribbon through. Let dry, then paint the hearts green on both sides.

3 TIE ON CLAY DECORATIONS Thread the narrow ribbon through the holes of one heart and tie a knot at the back of the heart to prevent it slipping off. Tie the narrow ribbon around the neck of the bag and draw tight. Now tie the thicker ribbon together around the ends of the narrow ribbon, just below the knot.

4 FINISH OFF Tie the thicker ribbon in a bow around the neck of the cellophane bag. Tease the top of the bag so that it looks attractive. Trim the ends of the ribbon on the diagonal to prevent the ends fraying.

christmas spice cookies

It's lots of fun making your own edible Christmas decorations or treats for a special birthday party. Just cut shapes out of a sweet biscuit dough, then have lots of fun decorating them with coloured icing and silver balls.

1 Put a bit of butter on a piece of kitchen paper and rub it over the baking trays to grease them.

2 Put the flour, cinnamon, ginger and mixed spice in the bowl of a food processor. Using an ordinary table knife, cut the butter into small pieces and add to the bowl of the processor.

3 Ask an adult to help you run the processor until the mixture looks like fine breadcrumbs.

4 Measure the honey into the bowl of the processor and, with adult help, run the processor until the mixture comes together to make a ball of dough.

5 Ask an adult to help you remove the blade from the bowl, then remove the dough from the bowl. Wrap the dough in clingfilm or greaseproof paper and put it into the fridge until it is firm enough to roll out – probably about 30 minutes.

6 Ask an adult to help you preheat the oven to 180°C (350°F) Gas 4.

7 Lightly sprinkle the work surface and a rolling pin with flour. Gently roll out the dough until it is about 5 mm thick. Cut out shapes using your cookie cutters. Gather up the trimmings into a ball, then roll out and cut more shapes. To make Christmas decorations to hang up, you'll need to make a small hole at the top of each cookie with a cocktail stick (make sure the hole is large enough to thread a ribbon through).

8 Arrange the shapes slightly apart on the baking trays. Ask an adult to help you put them in the oven to bake for about 10 minutes, or until golden. Ask an adult to help you carefully remove from the oven and put the trays onto a heatproof surface and leave to cool for 5 minutes. Gently transfer the cookies to a wire rack and leave until cold.

9 Decorate the cookies however you like: you could thread them with ribbon, then ice using coloured icing pens and silver balls. Leave until the icing is set, then hang them up. Eat your cookies as soon as possible or store them in an airtight container and eat within five days.

WHAT YOU WILL NEED
* 2 non-stick baking trays
* 175g unsalted butter, straight from the fridge, plus extra butter for greasing
* 300g plain flour
* 2 teaspoons ground cinnamon
* ½ teaspoon ground ginger
* ½ teaspoon ground mixed spice
* 6 tablespoons clear honey
* thin ribbon, thread or raffia, to hang
* icing pens and silver balls, to decorate
* a selection of shaped cookie cutters such as stars, Christmas trees, angels, bells and reindeer

makes about 24 cookies

snow shakers

Snow shakers make great gifts and children always enjoy making them. We used Christmas decorations inside ours, but your child may like to use small plastic animals or even to make their own decorations to put inside.

1 FILL JARS Use a jug to pour the distilled water into the jam jar. Fill it as full as possible. Add two teaspoons of glycerine, and half a teaspoon of detergent.

2 ADD GLITTER Spoon the glitter into the water. You will need approximately five or six teaspoons. White or silver glitter looks most similar to snow, although red or green or other bright colours can look very jolly and festive.

3 ATTACH DECORATION Use a blob of strong waterproof glue to securely stick the decoration to the inside of the jam-jar lid. It is advisable for an adult to do this if the child is young. Allow the glue to dry thoroughly according to the manufacturer's instructions.

4 SECURE LID Carefully place the lid on the top of the jam jar and screw tightly in place. The jam jar should be watertight, but you may wish to seal it around the edges with a layer of craft silicone sealant, which is available from good craft shops.

potato print wrapping paper

Potato printing is a traditional painting technique that is a favourite with kids of all ages. They can use cookie cutters to create pretty shapes, or an adult could use a sharp knife to cut out different shapes by hand.

1 CUT OUT SHAPE Cut the potato in half, making sure the surface of the potato is as flat as possible. Place the cookie cutter on a cutting board with the sharp edge facing upward. Press the potato firmly down onto the cutter, leaving the cookie cutter standing proud of the cut surface of the potato by about 5mm, so you can cut all the way around it.

2 CUT AWAY EDGES Ask an adult to cut away the edges of the potato using a sharp knife. This needs to be done very carefully, to make sure the star shape is as clear as possible. Press the potato down on a dry cloth to remove any excess moisture, which can make the paint watery.

3 APPLY PAINT Pour paint into a saucer and use the end of the sponge roller to apply the paint to the star shape. Don't apply too much paint to the potato, as this will make the design bleed. If you have applied too much, gently blot the potato on paper towels to remove the excess.

4 GET PRINTING Begin printing. To make sure the design prints clearly, use a gentle rocking motion, moving the potato from side to side without lifting it from the paper. This will apply the paint evenly, even if the cut surface of the potato is not flat. Continue to print the stars at evenly spaced intervals. Allow the paint to dry completely.

WHAT YOU WILL NEED

⊛ medium-sized potato
⊛ star-shaped cookie cutter
⊛ chopping board
⊛ sharp knife
(to be used by an adult only)
⊛ paper towels or dry cloth
⊛ paints in your chosen colours
⊛ saucers to hold the paints
⊛ sponge paint roller
⊛ plain white paper

nativity scene

A wonderful family keepsake that can be brought out every year, this nativity scene is made from Fimo coloured modelling clay. Each figure is based on a simple tube shape and decorated with touches of gold.

1 MAKE BABY Take some white modelling clay and roll out a bean shape about 3cm in length for the baby's body. If the modelling clay is hard, work it between the hands first to soften it, so it is easier to mould into shape.

3 MAKE CRIB Take the brown modelling clay and roll it into a bean shape measuring about 4cm in length and about 1.5cm in diameter. Use your thumb to press down and make an indentation in the crib. Roll two balls of brown modelling clay and press them flat to make the legs of the crib.

4 DECORATE WITH RAFFIA Use scissors to snip small pieces of raffia for the straw in the crib. Press the pieces of raffia firmly against the sides of the crib until they stick in place.

2 MAKE FACE Take a small piece of flesh-coloured modelling clay and roll it into a ball. Flatten it with your fingers to form a small round disc. Press the disc firmly onto the top of the body shape. Use tiny pieces of black clay to make the eyes and a mouth, and press them into position on the face.

7 ATTACH ARMS Make two small rolls of flesh-coloured clay for the arms and press them firmly against the front of the body. Use more small pieces of clay to form the gifts for the kings to carry, and press them into position between the arms at the front of the body.

5 MAKE OTHER FIGURES
Each figure for the nativity scene is made from a basic bean shape formed from clay and measuring approximately 5cm in length and 1.5cm in diameter. Then take a small piece of flesh-coloured clay, roll it into a ball and press it flat to form a round face. Using the same method, make a beard from brown clay and use tiny pieces of black clay for the eyes and mouth.

6 MAKE CLOAK To make the cloak, roll out a piece of clay to approximately 10cm long by 1cm wide. Fold it over the body and press firmly in place. If the cloak is too long, trim the ends with scissors.

8 FINISH OFF The kings' gifts and crowns are finished off with fine gold dust applied with a paintbrush. Lay the figure on its side while you apply the dust, to prevent it falling onto the rest of the figure.

orange pomanders

These traditional scented pomanders made from oranges and decorated with cloves have been associated with Christmas since medieval times. Their sweetly spicy smell makes them welcome gifts for family and friends, but they are also pretty decorations to hang in the home or can be used to scent cupboards.

1 MARK RIBBON POSITIONS
Use the ballpoint pen to mark out the ribbon positions around the orange. (The ribbon is wrapped round the orange in the shape of a cross.) Use the awl to pierce holes for the cloves on the four quarters of the orange. Awls are very sharp, so it is advisable for an adult to pierce the holes.

2 INSERT CLOVES Carefully push the cloves into the orange. The tops of the cloves can be quite brittle, so push them in gently. Continue to push the cloves into the orange until all four quarters are covered.

3 FIX RIBBON Wrap a length of ribbon around the orange so the ends overlap at the bottom of the orange. Snip the ribbon and hold the first piece in place as you wrap another length around the orange. Trim any trailing ribbon ends. Now push a pin through the ends of the ribbon to hold it securely in place.

4 FINISH OFF Thread a length of ribbon through the top of the crossed ribbon on the orange and tie the ends together. Tie a knot in the ribbon about 5cm from the top of the orange to form a loop. Now thread a further length of ribbon through the top of the ribbon and tie into a pretty bow to finish.

WHAT YOU WILL NEED

- ✪ paper and pencil
- ✪ scissors
- ✪ coloured felt
- ✪ pins
- ✪ pinking shears
- ✪ 15cm red ricrac per decoration
- ✪ needle
- ✪ matching cotton thread
- ✪ polyester stuffing
- ✪ glue
- ✪ assorted pearl buttons, to decorate

hanging felt stars

Cut from red and green felt using pinking shears, these jolly tree decorations are an ideal easy sewing project for little fingers. We decorated the star shapes with pretty buttons and hung them from ricrac braid loops.

1 MAKE TEMPLATE Trace the star template on page 152 onto a piece of paper and cut it out.

2 DRAW AROUND TEMPLATE Fold the felt in half, as you will need two star shapes per decoration. Use a pencil to draw around the star motif on the felt fabric (it may be easier if you first pin the star motif to the felt to keep it in place).

3 CUT OUT Using pinking shears, carefully cut all the way around the star shape, making sure you are cutting through both layers of fabric. The pinking shears give a zigzag effect to the edges and, if you are using cotton or linen, will prevent the fabric from fraying. If you are making more than one star decoration, it is a good idea to cut them all out at one time.

4 ATTACH LOOP Fold a 15cm length of ricrac braid in half and place between the two layers of felt at the top of one of the points. Thread the needle. Push the needle through the two layers of felt, sandwiching the loop between them, and make two or three stitches to secure the hanging loop.

5 STITCH TOGETHER Continue stitching all the way around the points of the star, using small running stitches about 3mm from the edge. Stitch around five sides of the star, but leave the sixth side open for the stuffing.

6 STUFF HEART Carefully push the stuffing into the opening. You may need to use the end of a knitting needle or a pencil to make sure that the stuffing is pushing right into all the points of the star.

7 STITCH OPENING CLOSED Hold the two layers of felt together and stitch the opening closed, again using small running stitches 3mm from the edges of the fabric. Cast off the stitching by making two or three stitches together, and snip the loose ends of the cotton.

8 FINISH OFF Use neat dabs of glue to stick the buttons to the front of the star decoration, then leave to dry completely. You may wish to glue buttons to the other side of the decoration (you will need extra buttons for this).

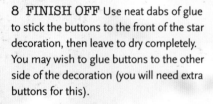

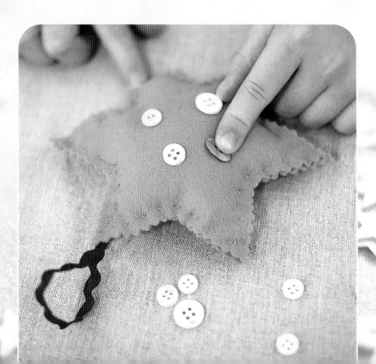

chocolate brownies

These delicious chocolate brownies filled with chunks of chocolate are given a festive touch with stencilled Christmas tree motifs made using icing sugar. If you can resist the temptation of eating them yourself, they make great gifts for teachers, family and friends.

1 MIX INGREDIENTS Preheat the oven to 160°C (325°F) Gas 3. Cut a 25cm square of foil and use it to line the base and sides of the tin. Melt the butter in a saucepan over a low heat. Crack the eggs into a mixing bowl. Pour in the sugar, then add the vanilla. Stir well with a wooden spoon. Pour in the melted butter and stir. Set a sieve over the mixing bowl and sift the cocoa and flour onto the egg mixture. Stir well.

2 ADD CHOCOLATE Break the chocolate into small chunks and add to the bowl. Stir until just mixed, then spoon the mixture into the foil-lined tin. Ask an adult to help you put the brownie mix into the oven. They will take about 40 minutes to cook in the centre of the oven. To test if they are ready, push a cocktail stick into one, then pull it out. If the stick is clean, they are ready; if it's sticky, leave them for another 5 minutes.

3 CUT OUT STENCIL Ask an adult to remove the tin from the oven, as it will be very hot. Leave the tin to cool on a wire rack. When completely cold, remove the brownies from the tin, peel off the foil and cut into 16 squares. Trace the Christmas tree stencil on page 155 on paper and cut out the Christmas tree shape from the middle. This is your stencil.

4 FINISHING Place the stencil on top of a brownie and sift icing sugar over the stencil and brownie. Carefully remove the stencil to reveal the Christmas tree motif. Repeat until all the brownies are decorated.

WHAT YOU WILL NEED

- ✪ aluminium foil
- ✪ 20cm square cake tin
- ✪ 140g unsalted butter
- ✪ 4 large eggs
- ✪ 320g caster sugar
- ✪ 1 teaspoon vanilla essence
- ✪ 75g cocoa powder
- ✪ 140g plain flour
- ✪ 100g milk chocolate
- ✪ paper for stencil
- ✪ icing sugar to decorate

makes 16 brownies

angel tree topper

Decorate simple cones of card with a sprinkling of sparkling glitter and a pompom to create these pretty tree-top angels complete with a metallic pipe-cleaner halo and wings. Quick, easy and effective!

1 DRAW AROUND PLATE
Place the plate on the silver card and draw around half of it to create a semi-circle for the cone. Cut out.

2 APPLY GLITTER Use glue to draw a scalloped or zigzag line all around the curved edge of the semicircular piece of card. Sprinkle silver glitter generously over the glue and leave for a few minutes. Shake off any excess glitter and allow the glue to dry completely.

3 FORM CONE SHAPE Form the card semicircle into a cone shape (folding it gently in half and making a slight crease at the centre of the card makes it a bit easier to form a cone). Use a stapler to hold the edges of the card together.

WHAT YOU WILL NEED

- ✪ 25cm-diameter plate as template for cone shape
- ✪ silver card
- ✪ pencil
- ✪ scissors
- ✪ glue
- ✪ silver glitter
- ✪ stapler
- ✪ silver pipe-cleaner
- ✪ pompom for head
- ✪ blue and pink 3-D fabric paint pens
- ✪ gold pipe-cleaner

4 MAKE WINGS Use the silver pipe-cleaner to form the angel's wings. Twist the two ends over to form a figure of eight.

5 ATTACH WINGS Apply a dab of glue to the centre of the wings and glue them to the back of the cone, about 3cm down from the top. Allow glue to dry completely.

6 GLUE ON POMPOM HEAD
Either use a ready-made pompom or make your own following the instructions on pages 28–29. Glue the pompom to the top of the cone and leave to dry.

7 DRAW FACE Use 3-D fabric paint pens in pink and blue to carefully draw the angel's eyes and mouth onto the pompom. Leave to dry.

8 FINISH OFF For the halo, bend a gold pipe-cleaner into a circular shape with a diameter of about 3cm. Twist the ends together to secure, and glue it to the top of the pompom head to finish.

christmas stocking

Create this pretty Shaker-style stocking in cream wool and decorate with a simple heart and mother-of-pearl button. You could even make one for each member of the family and tie on card name tags.

1 CREATE A TEMPLATE Trace the stocking template on page 155 onto a piece of paper. Now enlarge it on a photocopier at 200 per cent to make it the right size. Cut out the template. Fold the cream wool fabric in half and pin the template to the fabric. Cut out the stocking pieces.

2 CUT OUT HEART MOTIF Trace the heart template on page 155 onto a piece of paper and cut it out. Pin the template to the felt and cut out a heart shape to decorate the front of the stocking.

3 TACK HEART TO STOCKING Thread the needle with white cotton and tack the heart to the front stocking piece.

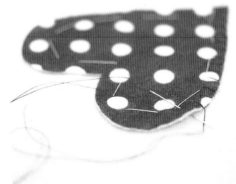

4 BLANKET-STITCH HEART Now thread the needle with red cotton and work small blanket stitches all the way around the heart motif. When you have finished, carefully remove the tacking. Now use a dab of glue to stick the pearl button to the very centre of the heart.

WHAT YOU WILL NEED

- paper and pencil
- scissors
- 40cm cream fabric (137cm wide)
- pins
- red felt for heart (15cm x 15cm)
- needle
- white thread
- red thread
- glue
- pearl button
- red embroidery thread
- 20cm gingham fabric (137cm wide)
- 10cm gingham ribbon

5 STITCH STOCKING TOGETHER With right sides facing, tack the two stocking pieces together. Turn right side out. Thread a needle with the red embroidery thread and work blanket stitch all the way around the edges of the stocking, leaving the top edges of the stocking open. Press flat using a warm iron (it is advisable for an adult to do this).

6 MAKE GINGHAM BORDER Take the piece of gingham fabric. Fold it in half lengthways, with right sides together, and stitch the side seams together using small running stitches. Turn right side out and press flat using an iron (it is advisable for an adult to do this).

7 STITCH GINGHAM TO STOCKING Turn a 1cm hem to the inside of the gingham and press flat. Tuck about 8cm of the gingham fabric inside the stocking and fold the remainder of the fabric over the top of the stocking, with the hemmed edge on the outside. Sew small running stitches all around the top of the gingham fabric to hold it in place.

8 SEW ON HANGING LOOP

Fold the piece of gingham ribbon in half to form a loop, and stitch it to the inside of the gingham fabric at the back seam of the stocking.

templates

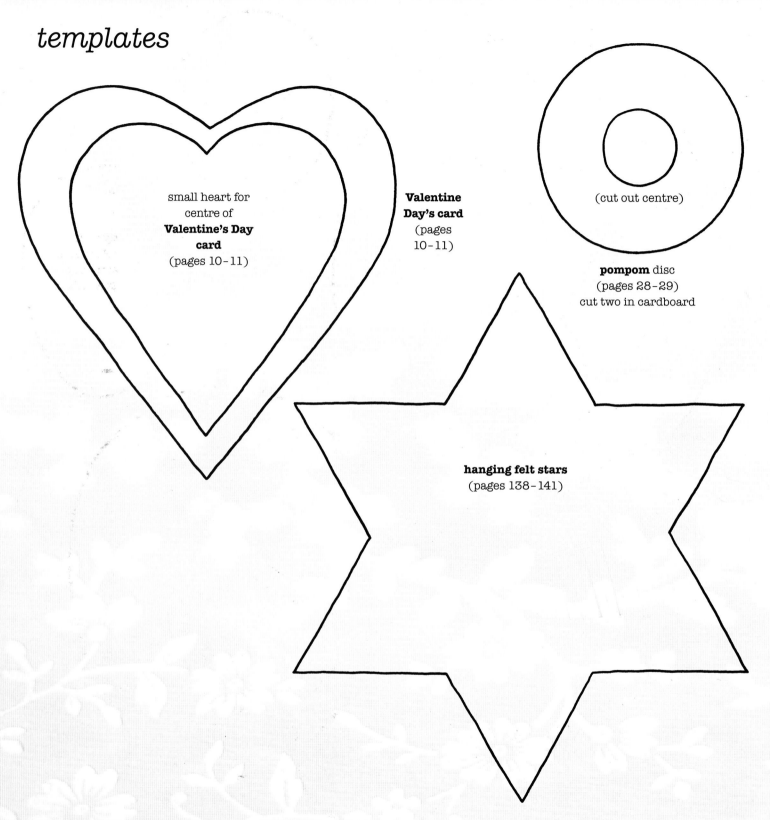

small heart for centre of **Valentine's Day card** (pages 10-11)

Valentine Day's card (pages 10-11)

(cut out centre)

pompom disc (pages 28-29) cut two in cardboard

hanging felt stars (pages 138-141)

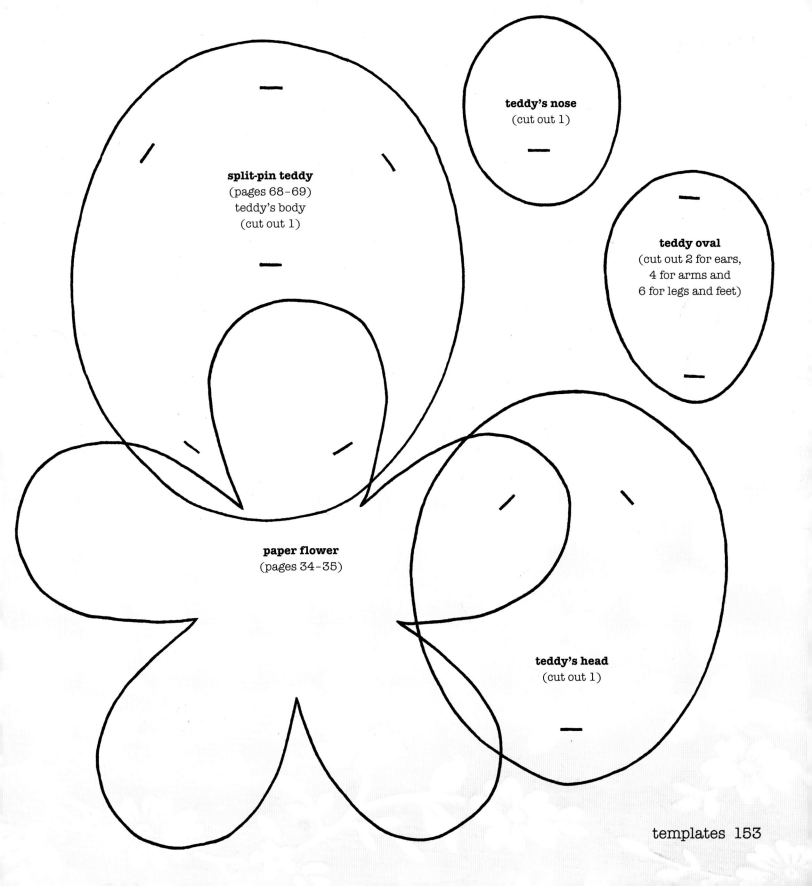

teddy's nose
(cut out 1)

teddy oval
(cut out 2 for ears,
4 for arms and
6 for legs and feet)

split-pin teddy
(pages 68–69)
teddy's body
(cut out 1)

paper flower
(pages 34–35)

teddy's head
(cut out 1)

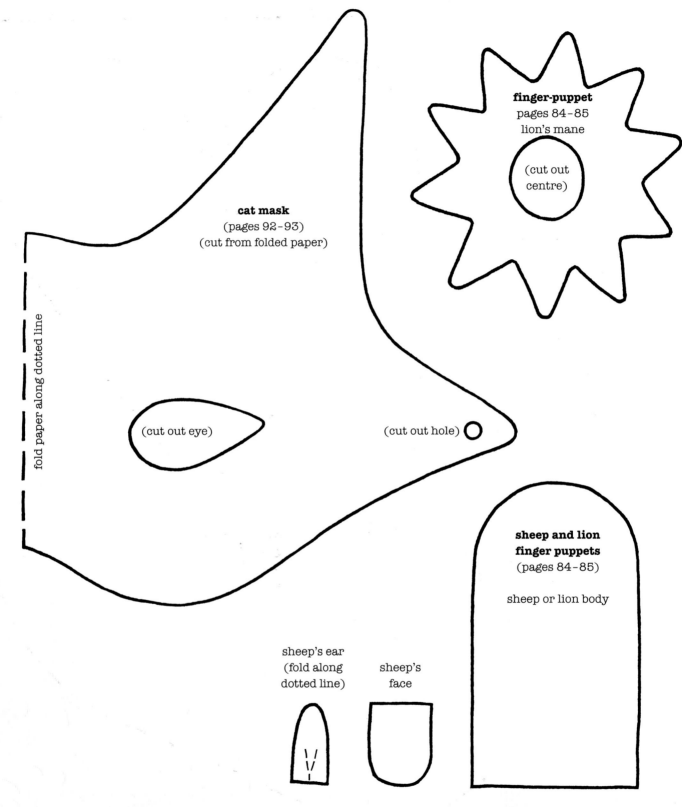

finger-puppet
pages 84–85
lion's mane

(cut out
centre)

cat mask
(pages 92–93)
(cut from folded paper)

fold paper along dotted line

(cut out eye)

(cut out hole)

**sheep and lion
finger puppets**
(pages 84–85)

sheep or lion body

sheep's ear
(fold along
dotted line)

sheep's
face

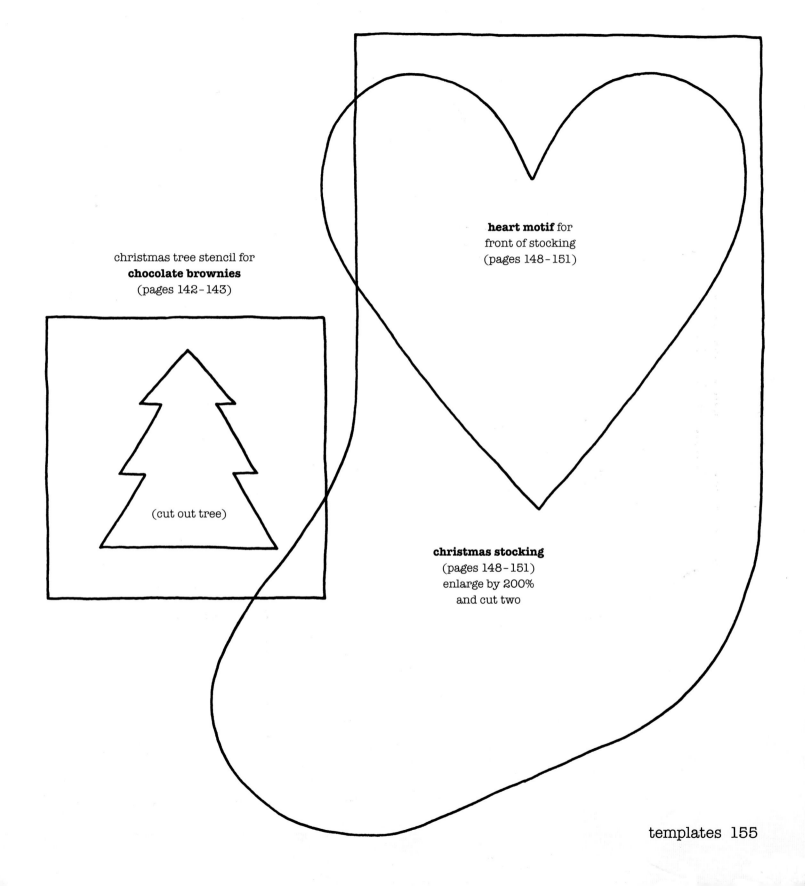

christmas tree stencil for
chocolate brownies
(pages 142–143)

(cut out tree)

heart motif for
front of stocking
(pages 148–151)

christmas stocking
(pages 148–151)
enlarge by 200%
and cut two

templates 155

stockists

CALICO CRAFTS
www.calicocrafts.co.uk
Online crafts specialist with large stock of crafting materials, including vintage-style labels that are ideal for découpage projects.

CATH KIDSTON
51 Marylebone High Street
London W1U 5HW
020 7935 6555
Visit www.cathkidston.co.uk for details of your nearest store.
Pretty vintage-style fabrics.

CONFETTI
80–81 Tottenham Court Road
London W1T 4TE
0870 774 7177
www.confetti.co.uk
Ribbons, feathers and sequins plus wrapping paper, blank cards and envelopes.

CREATIONS ART AND CRAFTS MATERIALS
01326 555777
www.ecreations.co.uk
Online craft store selling air-drying modelling clay in a wide variety of colours, rubber stamps and stencils, paints, glue and more.

THE DOVER BOOKSHOP
18 Earlham Street
London WC2H 9LG
020 7836 2111
www.doverbooks.co.uk
Permission and copyright-free images for découpage, or to make cards and gift wrap.

EARLY LEARNING CENTRE
Call 0870 535 2352 or visit www.elc.co.uk for details of your nearest store.
Their large craft section includes funky-coloured paints, different-sized paintbrushes, felt-tip pens, scissors, glitter pens, glue, pompoms, coloured feathers and simple stencils – great for younger children who enjoy art and craft.

ELLS & FARRIER
20 Beak Street
London W1F 9RE
020 7629 9964
www.creativebeadcraft.co.uk
The huge selection of beads available on the website includes wood, glass, rocaille, pearl and crystal designs, as well as feathers, sequins and tiny glass beads.

THE ENGLISH STAMP COMPANY
www.englishstamp.com
Traditional wooden stamps, including many designs that will appeal to kids, such as fairies and animals, as well as a good selection of Christmassy stamps in various sizes. Also ink pads and blank card.

GREAT LITTLE TRADING CO.
Call 0870 850 6000 or visit www.gltc.co.uk for a catalogue.
A wide selection of craft-related items, including ready-mixed paints, art folders, table-top easels and fun craft kits for kids.

HOBBYCRAFT
Westway Cross Shopping Park
Greenford Road
London UB6 0UW
0800 027 2387
Visit www.hobbycraft.co.uk for details of your nearest store.
Craft superstores carrying ribbons, pompoms, air-drying clay, Fimo modelling clay, blank cards and envelopes, Christmas stamps and ink stamp pads, sequins, buttons and beads, plus much more.

HOMECRAFTS DIRECT
0116 269 7733
www.homecraftsdirect.co.uk
Tinsel pipe-cleaners, plain wooden frames and cracker snaps, as well as all the necessary craft staples, including crêpe paper, plain and coloured doilies, glue sticks, glue guns, fabric paints, air-drying clay, Fimo modelling clay, ready-to-decorate face masks and instant papier-mâché mix.

HOPEFISH
www.hopefish.co.uk
Craft kits and arts and crafts supplies – great for craft-themed birthday parties.

IKEA
Visit www.ikea.com for a catalogue or details of your nearest store.
Good selection of wooden boxes and files and plain picture frames in unfinished wood that are ready for painting and decorating. Also seasonal selections of fun decorations, wrapping paper and cards.

JANE ASHER PARTY CAKES AND
SUGARCRAFT
24 Cale Street
London SW3 3QU
020 7584 6177
www.jane-asher.co.uk
Excellent selection of novelty-shaped cookie
cutters in both metal and plastic, plus cake
decorations, cake frills, a variety of pretty
paper doilies and coloured cake cases in
many different sizes.

JOHN LEWIS
Visit *www.johnlewis.com* for details of your
nearest store.
John Lewis haberdashery departments offer
embroidery threads and cottons in many
colours, as well as craft essentials, including
felt, pipe-cleaners, ribbons, ricrac braid,
pretty buttons and sequins.

LAKELAND LTD
Visit *www.lakelandlimited.com* for details
of your nearest store.
Crafting products available both via mail
order and on the web, including blank cards
and envelopes, ribbons, card kits and a huge
selection of decorative stamps and inks.

MACCULLOCH & WALLIS
25–26 Dering Street
London W1S 1AT
020 7629 0311
www.macculloch-wallis.co.uk
Vast selection of fabrics, including boiled
wool, wool and felt, as well as lace, ribbons
and ricrac and other braids sold by the metre.

MUJI
Visit *www.muji.co.uk* for details of your
nearest store.
Plain boxes and notecards, which are idea for
covering or découpage. Also pens, pencils
and scissors.

PAPERCHASE
213 Tottenham Court Road
London W1T 7PS
020 7467 6200
Visit *www.paperchase.co.uk* for details of
your nearest store.
Large selection of hand-made papers, crêpe
and tissue paper and metallic card, fabric-
covered books and photograph albums. Also
3-D paint, glitter glue pens, and blank cards
and envelopes in many colours and sizes.

VV ROULEAUX
6 Marylebone High Street
London W1M 3PB
020 7224 5179
Visit *www.vvrouleaux.com* for details of
their other stores.
A vast selection of ribbons, from taffeta and
velvet to embroidered cotton, plus
pompoms, pretty trims, feather butterflies
and fabric flowers.

SELWYN-SMITH STUDIOS
148 High Street
Teddington
Middlesex TW11 8HZ
020 8973 0771
Paper, pens, pencils and brushes.

THE STENCIL LIBRARY
Stocksfield Hall
Northumberland
NE43 7TN
01661 844844
www.stencil-library.com
Decorative stencils ranging from simple
festive shapes to more complicated designs,
plus stencil paints and brushes. Paints can
be used on walls, furniture and fabric.

TOYS R US
Visit *www.toysrus.co.uk* for details of
your nearest store.
A wide selection of colourful art and craft
kits that make great gifts.

THE WIMBLEDON SEWING & CRAFT
SUPERSTORE
296–312 Balham High Road
London SW17 7AA
020 8767 0036
www.craftysewer.com
Everything from decorative beads and
sequins to blank metallic card, Fimo
modelling clay, fabric dyes, felt, pompoms,
wool, buttons and pipe-cleaners.

picture credits

PHOTOGRAPHY

VANESSA DAVIES

Pages 1–6, 10–11, 12–13, 14–15, 16–17, 18 background, 20–21, 26–27, 28–29, 32–33, 34–35, 40–41, 46–47, 49, 50–51, 52–53, 54–55, 58–59, 64–65, 68–69, 72–73, 80–81, 84–85, 86–87, 92–93, 94–95, 96–97, 116–117, 118–119, 128–129

POLLY WREFORD

Pages 4 background, 7 background, 8, 9, 10–11 background, 12–13 background, 18–19, 22–25, 30–31, 32–33 background, 36–39, 42–45, 48, 50–51 background, 52–53 background, 56–57, 60–61, 62–63, 66–67, 70–71, 72–73 background, 74–75, 76–77, 78–79, 80–81 background, 82–83, 86–87 background, 88–89, 90–91, 92–93 background, 96–97 background, 98–99, 100–101, 102–103, 104–105, 106–107, 108–109, 110–111, 112–113, 114–115, 120–121, 122–123, 124–125, 126–127, 130–131, 132–135, 136–137, 138–141,142–143, 144–147, 148–151

index

a
angel tree topper 144–7
animals
    pine cone animals 114–15
    split pin animals 68–9
annuals, colourful 70–71
apron, printed 18–19

b
bags, lavender 102–3
balsa wood, modelling with 58–9
bird feeders
    birdseed feeder 88–9
    peanut heart 78–9
books, covering 80–81
bowls: Mother's Day gift 12–13
brownies, chocolate 142–3

c
cards
    felt motif cards 120–21
    Valentine's Day card 10–11
cat mask 92–3
    template 154
chocolate brownies 142–3
Christmas tree template 155
Christmas spice cookies 126–7
Christmas stocking 148–51
    template 15
clay, modelling with 86–7
colourful annuals 70–71
cookies, Christmas spice 126–7
covering books 80–81
cress eggheads 30–31
crystallised pansies 66–7

d
decorations
    orange tree decorations 110–11
    twig decorations 108–9
découpage 32–3
dinosaur, papier mâché 40–41

e
eggs
    cress eggheads 30–31
    painted eggs 20–21

f
fans, funky 50–51
Father's Day gift 72–3
felt motif cards 120–21
finger puppets 84–5
    template 154
finger- and hand-painting 118–19
flowers
    colourful annuals 70–71
    crystallised pansies 66–7
    paper flowers 34–5
    pressing flowers 52–3
food
    chocolate brownies 142–3
    Christmas spice cookies 126–7
    cress eggheads 30–31
    crystallised pansies 66–7
    gingerbread people 26–7
    peppermint creams 122–3
funky fans 50–51

g
garden tote 22–5

gardening
  colourful annuals 70–71
  garden tote 22–5
  harvesting herbs 62–63
  herb planter 60–61
  pretty plant labels 74–5
  pretty seed packets 100–101
gingerbread people 26–7

h
Halloween hat 96–7
hanging felt stars 138–41
  template 152
harvest wreath 90–91
harvesting herbs 62–3
hat, Halloween 96–7
hearts
  peanut heart 78–9
  Valentine's Day card 10–11
herbs
  harvesting herbs 62–3
  herb planter 60–61

i
indoor garden 82–3

k
keyrings: Father's Day gift 72–3

l
lantern, pumpkin 104–5
lavender bags 102–3

m
mask, cat 92–3

mirror-image painting 94–5
modelling
  modelling with balsa wood 58–9
  modelling with clay 86–7
Mother's Day gift 12–13

n
nativity scene 132–5
necklace, seed 98–9
nesting box, wooden 40–45

o
orange pomanders 136–7
orange tree decorations 110–11

p
painted eggs 20–21
painted pots 56–7
painted stones 54–5
painting
  finger- and hand-painting 118–19
  mirror-image painting 94–5
pansies, crystallised 66–7
paper chains 116–17
paper flowers 34–5
  template 153
paper snowflakes 112–13
paper windmills 14–15
papier mâché
  Mother's Day gift 12–13
  papier mâché dinosaur 40–41
peanut heart 78–9
peppermint creams 122–3

pine cone animals 114–15
plant labels, pretty 74–5
planter, herb 60–61
pomanders, orange 136–7
pompoms 28–9
  template 153
pot pourri 124–5
potato-printing
  potato print wrapping paper 130–31
  printed apron 18–19
pots, painted 56–7
pressing flowers 52–3
pretty plant labels 74–5
pretty seed packets 100–101
printed apron 18–19
pumpkin lantern 104–5
puppets
  finger puppets 84–5
  wooden-spoon puppets 46–7

s
seed necklace 98–9
seed packets, pretty 100–101
snow shakers 128–9
snowflakes, paper 112–13
split-pin animals 68–9
stars, hanging felt 138–41
stocking, Christmas 148–51
stockists 156–7
stones, painted 54–5

t
t-shirt, tie-dye 64–5
templates

cat mask 154
Christmas stocking 155
Christmas tree (for chocolate brownies) 155
finger-puppet 154
hanging felt stars 152
pompom disc 153
sheep and lion finger puppets 154
Valentine's Day card 152
tie-dye t-shirt 64–5
tin can windchime 36–9
tote, garden 22–5
twig decorations 108–9

v
Valentine's Day card 10–11
  template 152

w
weaving 16–17
windchime, tin can 36–9
windmills, paper 14–15
wooden nesting box 40–45
wooden-spoon puppets 46–7
wrapping paper, potato print 130–31
wreath, harvest 90–91

acknowledgements

Thanks to the Norfolk Lavender Company for supplying the lavender, to J. Arthur Bowers for supplying the compost used in the gardening projects, and to Hobbycraft for supplying a wonderful selection of paper, fabrics, ribbons and other items for many of the projects.

Thank you also to the models who appear in the photographs in this book, including Ahana, Aimee, Alessandra, Alissia and Saskia, Anna and Jessica, Archie and Ollie, Archie, Arthur, Asha, Cameron, Chanelle and Ayeisha, Ella and Ivo, Ella, Eva, Eve, Georgia, Gus and Kit, Harriet, Havana and Hassia, Jack and Gabriella, Jack, Jessica, Jordan, Kaan, Katie, Lilee, Louis, Millie, Olivia, Oscar, Tabitha, Tahiti and William and James.